Toward Fascist America

2021: The Year that launched American Fascism

Charles Moscowitz

Books by Charles Moscowitz

We are all Socialists Now
God is God
The Nazi Connection to Islamic Terrorism
Islamo-Communism
The Socialist Bible
Bible Tabula Rasa
A Whig Manifesto
The Art and Science of American Money
On the Jewish Question: Karl Marx, anti-Semitism and the War against the West
Assassination Conspiracy in America
Was Hitler a Leftist
ACORN: The Takeover of America
Communism is not Dead
Apostles of Evolution
The counter-Fabians
The War against Judaism
The Revolutionary Mind and the counter-Revolution
American Testament
Barney Frank and the Law of Unintended Consequences

Charles Moscowitz Live / Mon-Fri 12 – 1 pm ET

YouTube
iTunes
Spotify
iHeartRadio
Spreaker
Google Play
Stitcher

Contact Charles Moscowitz:

charlesmoscowitz@gmail.com   (617) 271-5044

Introduction

I am an American Jew. I have been thinking about and studying Nazism and the Holocaust for over a half century, since my childhood. I remember as a young kid listening to my grandparents, my aunts and uncles, taking around the table about Hitler and the Holocaust. As a teenager I read what I would still contend is the most definitive book on the subject which is *The Rise and Fall of the Third Reich* by William L. Shrier who was a CBS correspondent in Berlin in the years leading up to World War II. I have since authored three books myself that include an examination of the politics and philosophy of Nazism and I have, over several decades, interviewed numerous authors and intellectuals on the topic.

Now that I have respectfully presented to you, dear reader, my modest bona fides, I will make a disclaimer which is that my views on this topic are colored by charged emotions and by levels of bias that might at times cloud my objectivity. I make no apology for this. I am particularly concerned over current events that might indicate authoritarian government overreach, the demonization of select individuals, and by extension select groups that might be singled out for political reasons as opposed to their specific actions and the censorship of legitimate opinion which I define broadly. My concerns over Nazism and the Holocaust have led me in the direction of mistrust of government, which also happens to be one of the guiding principles of the American political philosophy, and a concern over the proliferation and manifestation of ideas that might lead to the suppression of freedom.

In This short thesis I will present my contention that 2021 marks the beginning of a time that is dangerously similar to that of the first years of the 1933-1934 Nazi regime in Germany. I will compare the notorious Capitol incursion of January 6 and its reaction to the Reichstag fire which took place on February 27, 1933, four weeks after Adolf Hitler was sworn in as Chancellor of Germany, an event which was used by the newly installed Nazi regime as an excuse to suspend the constitution. I will examine the executive orders issued by the newly inaugurated Biden Administration in its first week on office with an eye toward what I perceive to be an authoritarian tendency. I will offer a brief study of the ascendancy of a culture, one that is becoming installed along with Biden, that encourages censorship by means of an informal collusion of government with the main instruments of communication. I will examine the accompanying phenomena that effectively condones and informally supports the denouncement of the opposition.

But…before we go there… a few definitions.

What is Fascism?

Broadly speaking, Fascism constitutes a political system that involves a merge between select corporations and a government oligarchy that is usually headed by either a figurehead or a strongman dictator. In the case of Fascist Italy, this was manifested as a government run by a council of corporations, one which replaced an elected Parliament, one that worked hand in glove with a dictator, and in the case of Italy that dictator was Benito Mussolini. This same model dominated the Nazi regime after the Reichstag fire and the effective suspension of the Reichstag. The corporations that made up the Italian council of corporations enjoyed the benefits of a legalized monopoly and this monopoly power was re-enforced by the dictator who wielded an absolute power that he derived from the consent of and the partnership with those select monopolistic corporations. The outward trappings of private ownership were left in place in Fascist Italy and in Germany but the real control over ownership, the economy, the culture, the media, and all of major institutions and conventions within the Fascist State resided with the corporate monopoly and its partnership with the dictatorial oligarchy.

Fascism is, by definition, National Socialism which is to say Socialism on the national as opposed to on the international level. National Socialism, as practiced by Fascist Italy and by Nazi Germany, differed from Bolshevik Communism which was a system of international socialism. Both systems are radical and revolutionary with the Fascist revolution primarily conducted within the State and the Communist revolution conducted both within the state and around the world. Both systems are atheist, and both systems hold utopian views that sanction the use of the apparatus of the state as a vehicle to be employed as a means to change human nature and to change humanity as a whole, allegedly for its own good. Both view human rights as emanating not from God, or from an external and objective force that is beyond the control of human manipulation, but rather that rights emanate from an enlightened clique of men who allegedly act for the common good.

Fascism differs from Communism in that Fascism permits the existence and, indeed, the advancement of select corporations working in tandem with the ruling oligarchy whereas Communism is a system by which the ruling oligarchy itself becomes the singular corporation that wields sole and undivided powers over the state. In this sense, Fascism is a less radical socialist system than is Communism which is why Fascism can and often is accurately described as to the right of Communism. While the Fascist state is often based on a reaction to the more radical and more socialist communist threat, both systems, while at war with each other both literally and philosophically, are nevertheless essentially the flip side of the same coin.

Thus…. Both Fascism and Communism are, by definition, to the left of the American form of government and those of the western democracies in general. Indeed, the American philosophy of government is the exact opposite of both the Fascist and Communist model. Fascism and Communism are both top-down political systems and, in a modernist revival of the ancient principle of the God-Emperor, and the medieval principle of the Devine Right of Kings, the Fascist and the Communist systems claim to be the source of rights which are granted, or which are withheld from the citizenry based upon fiat power and arbitrary whim.

What is Americanism?

The American system holds that all rights emanate from God which is to say that all rights emanate from an objective source of creation, a source that Thomas Jefferson referred to as the Creator in the American Declaration of Independence. In 1776, the American founding generation rejected the arbitrary earthly fiat power of the distant hereditary British Monarch, King George III, and by doing so they rejected the concept that rights emanate from the whim of a human source. The American theory of government would henceforth hold that all rights, indeed that all of existence itself emanates from a supernatural Creator and not from the man-made state and, as such, that the political state is created by human beings in an effort to preserve protect and defend those God given rights.

Unlike the two great Socialist experiments of the 20th Century, Fascism and Communism, the American political theory recognizes the inherently imperfect and, as such, the fallen nature of human beings and humanity as a whole. Americans are not by nature utopian but, rather, Americans are practical as Americans, as pragmatists, tend to work with that which is possible as opposed to trying to invent something that cannot exist. American political philosophy holds that individual freedom, the right of the individual to control his or her own life and destiny, is a right that exists within the parameters of what is possible to the individual.

Americans discovered the natural and indeed normal and existing virtues of limited government, a balance of powers, property, individual and local sovereignty, and a sense of personal responsibility based upon the moral restraints of faith, family, community, sobriety, propriety and good judgement. With the philosophical as well as the biblical understanding that God created each and every man and woman in his image, we Americans understand that we must place our own personal interests and our wellbeing first before we might be in a position to help others. In a reflection of the nature of all living things, Americans put themselves as well as their nation first among their fellows and among the nations of the world.

The War against Trump

As Americans, we ought to wake up to the true meaning of our creed by placing the interests of our nation first among all other nations of the world. This simple and obvious concept holds the key to understanding the core motivation behind the conscious enemies of President Trump as well as the enemies of the movement that he so valiantly and courageously championed. Indeed, by his rhetoric, by the example of his administration, by his biography and by his actions, Trump threatened to awaken the American citizen who is consciously beginning to grasp the meaning of his or her life and destiny and, as such, is developing an understanding of the conditions and the destiny of the American nation to which we are all invested. Donald Trump confronted the big lie which holds that in order to help others we have to sacrifice ourselves.

The conscious enemy consists of a loose and informal coalition of the top 1% wealthiest Americans and the top corporations along with those who hold commanding positions of influence in the media, academia, business, the cultural institutions and even religious institutions. This establishment tends to lean left politically favoring a socialistic view, but it may, from time to time, intersect with conservatives. This enemy tends to embrace a globalist conception which holds that such institutions and conventions as national sovereignty, borders, cultural identity and the sovereign nation-state itself are all anachronistic ideas that should be gradually and incrementally discarded. They tend to support free trade over free enterprise and, as such, they tend to oppose protection of the national economy and labor. They tend to resonate, at least unconsciously and culturally, with the Fascist and Communist utopian ideas of human perfectibility, absolute equality and world order.

These are the conscious and largely witting enemies of Donald Trump and his movement. They have both financial and ideological reasons for their enmity which leads them in a concerted effort to expunge Trump and his followers from public discourse. They were determined to stop Trump from holding office from the moment he stepped off the elevator at Trump Tower and announced his candidacy for the presidency right up until what I would argue was the most blatantly corrupt election in American history. They engaged in subversion, frame-ups, fake news and lies as they pushed any lever at their disposal. The unwitting and at least partially unconscious enemies of Trump, the masses of Trump haters, so to speak, were influenced by the constant and the almost daily drip of hate and false stories that emanated from most of the mainstream media every day of his presidency and which, indeed, is continuing even after he is out of office as this vicious agenda of destruction will likely follow Donald Trump to the grave and beyond.

The American people and their organizations and associations traditionally recognize the right of the citizen to exercise free speech and Americans expect to function in a relatively tolerant milieu, one that protects the open expression of legitimate and rational opinion to a high degree. In this context, political debate that might become fierce and might stretch credulity as means to win the political argument. Indeed, Americans understand that such arguments are the best means of discerning a closer approximation of truth and that this natural process is the primary reason why the founding fathers codified the 1st Amendment. Such fierce debate in to be expected in a free society where a great deal is at stake, where ideas and opinions matter, where ideas might become law or custom or, conversely, where good ideas might serve to undo and replace antiquated or erroneous ones. Ideas, once accepted or once rejected on a mass scale, might affect the course of freedom and might influence the philosophy and the way of life of our society for better or for worse.

In this context, a public issue emerged in America in 2016 due to the election of Donald J. Trump, one that I call Trump Derangement. (1.) My theory of Trump Derangement requires a brief examination of the personality of Donald Trump, (2.) the public policies that he promoted, and the negative reaction to that personality and those policies by what might euphemistically be referred to as the "eastern seaboard liberal establishment." I argue that the anti-Trump reaction of the liberal establishment and its constellation of followers, a reaction that is unprecedented in its rage and ferocity, one that this country has not seen since the decade before the Civil War, is primarily motivated by a major departure, a significant social shift away from a milieu that has dominated American public institutions, including both major American political parties, for at least the last half century.

The extreme reaction to President Trump and his movement was, I would argue, triggered by a general condition of derangement in those who were reacting as such. The term Trump Derangement (3.) is not used by me to in any way denigrate any person or group but, rather, the term is used by me to describe what I contend was a negative and extreme psycho-social reaction among those afflicted. The majority of Americans who opposed President Trump's policies, or those who disliked Donald Trump as a president or as a person, or those who opposed him for partisan reasons, it should be noted, were not necessarily part of the Trump Derangement phenomena but, rather, their opposition was more likely conventional. The tell-tale sign of Trump derangement was a consuming and obsessive hatred that was beyond reason or objectivity. In this context, the derangement, which finds its political locus in the globalist minded establishment, which consists of the top 1% wealthiest American citizens and corporations and their liberal-left cadres in the culture, media and academe, became an ideology in and of itself, almost an article of religious faith, by which every action by President Trump and, to varying degrees, every problem in society and even problems in personal life, including bad weather, might have been negatively tied to Trump and to his followers.

The first cause of what has become a public issue regarding Trump derangement is the fact that Donald Trump, the penultimate outsider, the first businessman elected President of the United States and the first president to have never held public office previously, a man who was an example of an alpha-male that harkens back to a previous era, does not speak and does not communicate in the authoritarian style that the establishment and its followers have come to expect. He does not speak in the usual clipped establishmentese, the vague British accent, a method which routinely utilizes euphemism, indirection, double-speak, lies, and the deceptive style of sophistic intellectualism. Unlike the typical establishment leader, Trump did not consult with experts and focus groups on order to find out who he was, and he did not depend too much on political handlers to help him decide what to say and how to say it, nor did he constantly read off a tele-prompter. President Trump spoke plainly which, putting aside his occasional lack of veracity, his lack of precision and clarity, or his tendency to embellish, comes across as honest to a fault. This factor, as much as any other, drives the establishment into a lather of rage.

Trump could be crude, he could be cruel and bombastic, and he often had the subtlety of a broken leg. While most politicians send out surrogates to do the dirty work of smearing opponents, Trump often took on the task himself. He conducted an end-run around the pundits and the media filters by getting his message directly to his fellow citizens, in his own voice, through his Twitter account which is why Twitter censored him in his last week in office. His use of social media transformed politics in the same way that FDR used radio broadcasts, his "fireside chats," and JFK used TV to his advantage. (4.) A billionaire businessman, Donald Trump largely spent his own money, and used his own experience and his own contacts as a media star to get elected which meant that he was not beholden to the usual establishment special interests and lobbyists. Trump could not be easily bought or controlled, and his actions could not be easily predicted. The idea of draining the swamp flew in the face of a liberal establishment in a manner that reminds me, metaphorically, of Guy Fawkes showing up at the Parliament with dynamite.

President Trump either ignored or attacked nostrums of political correctness that had become accepted social norms, ones that had come to dominate the high ground of our culture, nostrums that were selectively used as weapons against people or against groups that failed to genuflect to liberalism. Racism, discrimination, white supremacy, these all have been a negative part of the American milieu since the first colonists arrived on the American shore. Particularly since World War II, racial and ethnic barriers began to melt away at an accelerated rate as racism began to recede. Perhaps it is a testament to the success, albeit imperfect and there still is a long way to go, of the decline of racism that liberals insist upon resurrecting the old bugbear by means of what I would argue is the pseudo-science of micro-aggression. (5.) By this means, anyone who fails to bow to the liberal establishment runs the risk of being put under a proverbial microscope and examined for a racist gene. Indeed, the politicizing, the scientizing of racism has turned this genuine and serious social problem into a political football. The politicization of racism serves the dual purpose of obscuring the de-facto racist programs and ideas, emanating from the left, that have wracked havoc on the black family, the black church, black education, black culture, black entrepreneurialism and black economic advancement since the 1960's.

While President Trump challenged microaggressions, which constitute an informal form of tyranny, those afflicted with Trump derangement, many of whom themselves embrace extreme forms of racial, ethnic, gender and sexual identity politics, placed his every public utterance under the micro-aggression microscope. By this means, Trump derangement leads to a parsing of his words, usually out of context, and the manufacture of many self-serving scenarios that, in the de-facto sense, could be described as hoaxes. This fallacy of propaganda is destructive to the fabric of American society and the process is cynically utilized by conscious and witting enemies of Trump to divide constituencies and mobilize groups based upon prejudice and shared hatreds. (6.) Examples of this type of propaganda include the false and debunked portrayal of Trump as having mocked a disabled person, the false claim that Trump supported white supremacists and Nazis at the Charlottesville Virginia riots and the false claim that Trump supported a "Muslim ban." Indeed, these destructive articles of propaganda, pounded into the minds of all of us by the anti-Trump media, have become articles of faith for the Trump deranged and their unwitting followers. Trump's enemies employ the fallacy of dramatic instance by stringing together manufactured memes as a means to create a critical mass, the necessary atmosphere to support a false argument.

While the mainstream media often made normal mistakes in the past and, according to evidence gathered over time, the media tends to slant coverage in the direction that illustrates a liberal bias and a liberal culture, the level of bias, due to Trump derangement, crossed into the realm of what Trump accurately called fake news. Indeed, false stories became routine and part of the drum-beat used to delegitimize Trump and his movement. The result was a perceptible drop in journalistic standards and, conversely, a decline in public confidence in the honesty and dependability of the media. While hundreds of examples could be sited of this phenomena, I will confine myself to one example, albeit a minor one in the greater scheme of things, in order to illustrate my contention.

In July 2019, a local African-American politician from Georgia, Erica Thomas, claimed that a man told her to "go back" to her country because she had allegedly cut in front of him at the check-out counter at the local Walmart. This incident occurred after a massive media event a few days previous by which Trump had criticized a group of congresswoman, known as "the squad." The angle of the coverage of Trump's criticism of the squad was that it was motivated by the fact that two of the four congresswomen he criticized happened to be African-American. This contention fit neatly into the ongoing divisive and destructive narrative that Donald Trump had something against black men and women and other people of color, an article of faith for Trump derangement, a smear that many followers have actually come to believe. While Trump's comments were crude and needlessly belligerent, as Trump tends to be an equal-opportunity offender, the media reportage sidestepped the substance of his otherwise legitimate criticism of the so-called squad. Besides grabbing the opportunity to promote Trump as a racist, this side-step on the part of the media may have been a means by which to divert attention away from the legitimate issues that Trump raised, issues that were not helpful to the liberal narrative.

The man accused of a racially charged incident by the Georgia politician at Walmart turned out to be Hispanic and a liberal Democrat and Erica Thomas recanted her accusation when challenged. This recantation by Thomas, and this local story, did not stop the New York Times, the most influential newspaper in America, from publishing a feature story on this incident. (7.) Amazingly, the NYT included the fact that Thomas had recanted her story but, in a classic agit-prop style that typified the media assault on Trump, they saved the recantation for one sentence buried near the end of the article. The bombshell NYT report, no-doubt taking valuable space away from real news, was picked up by several mainstream media outlets including Time Magazine, USA Today, Newsweek and the Huffington Post.

As previously noted, the underlying cause of Trump derangement amongst the more witting members of the liberal establishment involves their concern over the principles that Trump articulates, principles that caused his election, an election that they conspire to undo. Those principles are captured in a simple slogan that he frequently used which was "America First." This is the type of slogan that candidates from both political parties have often used disingenuously in order to get elected, mainly because the slogan makes sense. In the case of Trump, the concern amongst the establishment was that he actually meant what he said. Trump's style of communication, as previously noted, is plain and sincere as opposed to politicians who use slogans for bumper-stickers, as means to manipulate and deceive the public by stoking emotion. Indeed, in a classic case of psychological projection, the enemies of Trump frame him as a liar with their fact-checks, which they often use to interrupt him in real time, yet, clearly, their real concern was when he told the truth.

Once the sophistries and the half-truths are stripped away, the sloganeering liberal establishment is often not interested in placing the interests of America first but, rather, they support an ideology and an agenda that is globalist, that includes unfettered free trade, that promotes an amalgamation of America into a world community, one that is un-democratic in terms of their support for rule by appointed bureaucrats and judges, and one that views such social institutions as national borders and private property as regressive anachronisms. President Trump, by appealing to the common sense of Americans, has tried to re-negotiate trade agreements in favor of American industry and labor. He sought to end American military embroilment in foreign wars by de-escalation and the insistence that allies pay for their own defense. He reduced onerous domestic regulation and he worked to secure the national border. The liberal establishment fears that Trump might wake up the giant beast, the American people, to an awareness of the importance of placing the national interest as well as their own personal interests first as a matter of culture and as a matter of policy.

Thus, enters Trump derangement, the need to demonize President Trump and anyone who dares to support his presidency and his movement. Trump represents a move away from the old regressive socialistic authoritarian past and toward a future where individual rights are honored first and foremost. This is why the opposition to Trump is so fierce and so deranged. It is normal, indeed it is laudable, for citizens to oppose presidents on political and partisan grounds. The opposition to Trump, however, is not normal. It is not normal for me to be told in advance that a family Thanksgiving dinner, held immediately after the 2016 election, is to be a "Trump free zone." It is not normal for College students to go to safe-rooms, after the election, where they can play with playdough and receive counseling as happened at Tufts University and elsewhere. It is not normal for a president to have to undergo a three-year investigation, one that was supported by a drum-beat of hysterical conspiracy theories from the mainstream media, only to find out at the end of the day that the whole thing was based on a hoax, at best, and possibly seditious activity and an attempted coup at worst.

Trump derangement has taken a major toll on the American psyche and on American society in general. (9.) It has legitimized and normalized a mainstream media that regularly and brazenly twists the truth in the service of an ideological agenda. It has given a pass, for example, to police actions by which a 21-member Swat team, with machine-guns drawn and with CNN filming outside, can arrest a harmless old man who has no criminal record, Roger Stone, on a minor process crime. A large segment of the public, having been conditioned by four years of the nonstop drip…drip…drip effect of propaganda, delivered in the style of Chinese water torture, maniacally cheered as Stone was taken away in his nightgown and pushed into a police wagon on national television. It has allowed and it has justified innuendo, rumor, and outright lies to become ingrained into the public consciousness as fact which has sown deep and possibly permanent divisions that may take generations to overcome. Hopefully, enough Americans will wake up in time to the danger before the derangement, which continues to march on even with Trump gone, searching for more targets to destroy, further engulfs greater and more vulnerable segments of our society.

The Capitol breach and the Reichstag Fire

As the situation stands today, as this short book goes to publication, we simply have no hard proof that the election of 2020 was stolen as, while there is a great deal of evidence that this was the case, there is nevertheless no hard proof. The question regarding the election will remain one that will hang out there like a dark cloud, one that will remain unanswered as a result of a breakdown in the system which itself raises suspicions. Either way, as we enter into the first months of the Joe Biden Administration, almost half of Americans, and a majority of Republicans, according to recent polls. continue to believe that the election was stolen from President Trump and, as such, stolen from the voters. (1.)

Indeed, the system that should have determined whether the election was stolen failed on several fronts. Firstly, and most fundamentally, the mainstream media refused to investigate the allegations of voter and ballot fraud in the six contested states. They refused to send in investigative reporters, and they failed to interview the hundreds of people who filed affidavits, sworn testimony, claiming that they had witnessed improprieties of various sorts. Big Tech shadow banned this information while reducing if not blocking information during the campaign that might have been detrimental to Biden as was the case with the FBI investigation of Hunter Biden and their possession of his now infamous laptop. Those who raised questions about the possibility of election fraud were mocked and demeaned. Thus, in many ways both overt and subtle, big media and big tech put their thumb on the scale to help Biden both during the campaign and during the period of contestation after the election.

Secondly, four states where the election was contested, Pennsylvania, Michigan, Wisconsin and Georgia, and possibly other states as well, had created election laws, under the guise of the COVID-19 19 pandemic emergency, without going through the constitutional process of having those laws debated and voted on by the respective state legislatures. The US Constitution clearly delegates the authority to make election laws to the state legislatures. Yet, in those four states, governors, secretaries of state, state judges, possibly others, were making laws right up to the eve of the election and in the case of Pennsylvania even after the election.

Thirdly, state and federal judges, including the Supreme Court, refused to hear the over fifty cases that were filed claiming evidence of voter and ballot fraud. All of these cases, except one, were dismissed on technicalities which meant that the evidence was not heard in its proper venue, a courtroom, where it might have been vetted either way. The only case that was heard was in Wisconsin where the judge, after hearing the case and agreeing that over one hundred ballots were likely case unlawfully, nevertheless refused to rule on the case under the contention that to do so might effect the results of the election. The Supreme Court refused to hear the case of Texas vs Pennsylvania, a case in which Texas claimed that by unlawfully passing election laws, without the opportunity for the people of Pennsylvania to express their will through their legislative representatives, Pennsylvania had compromised the integrity of the voters of Texas by interfering in the election. This case was dismissed on the grounds that one state had no right to sue another state even though this has happened before and that the Supreme Court would be the only venue by which such a case might be heard.

And so, after all the normal appropriate venues for examining and deliberating the question of voter fraud had failed, the court of last resort, the US Congress, became the final hope for hearing the evidence. The Constitution sets January 6th as the date by which a joint session of Congress, both houses, formally convene in an election year and count the electors from each state which determines who the next president will be. At that time, as had happened in the past, any state election that is contested would have the opportunity to present evidence. Seven states elected alternative delegations than the ones that had been certified for Biden. Each contested state, after a formal request was jointly requested by at least one representative and one senator, would be allotted two hours to make their presentation. At the conclusion of the presentation, the Vice President of the United States, acting in the capacity as President of the joint session of Congress, would hold the plenary power to decide which contested delegation of electors would be recognized and counted or he could simply choose not to recognized either delegation altogether.

If enough delegations are not recognized, neither presidential candidate garners enough delegates, with 270 required, to win the election. In that case, the election is decided by a special session of Congress made up of 50 delegates with each state legislature appointing one delegate. This would mean that, for example, California and Rhode Island would hold the same power to elect the president. Given the fact that 31 state legislatures are controlled by the Republican Party, this would almost have guaranteed, in this scenario, that Trump would have been elected president.

President Trump had urged Vice President Mike Pence, who held the plenary authority as presiding president of the congressional assembly, to send the delegates back to the seven contested states where the respective legislatures would then hold the constitutional authority to certify either a Biden or a Trump delegation. This assertion was based upon the political theory that since the US Constitution grants the state legislatures the responsibility to make election laws and, as such, to regulate their elections, than those same legislatures would decide on the outcome. The problem with this theory is that state legislatures had not used those powers, as granted to them by the constitution, for many decades and most legislators had no idea that hey held such powers. (2.)

At the assembly, the states are called out in alphabetical order which meant that Arizona would be the first contested state on the list to be called forth. Arizona was thus called, the election was contested by the required one representative and one senator, and the Arizona delegation, at last, began to present what I would describe as stunning and shocking evidence of systemic voter fraud. This process was supposed to be followed by six additional states and, with each state receiving the two-hour allotment of time per state, the process might very well have continued for several days.

Ahh…But…then…alas…. then came the incursion into the Capitol.

The Arizona presentation was interrupted, the session was disbanded, Congress adjourned, and the congressman left the scene. Congress would then reconvene later that day, near midnight, and Congress would then proceed, without the requisite hearings over the contested states and in the wee hours of the morning, to gavel Biden in. This, effectively, constituted a soft coup d'état. There was no reason why Congress could not have reconvened the next day during regular hours where the public and the media could have witnessed the proceedings. There was no reason why the hearings over the 7 contested states could not have proceeded normally and the states could not have thus had their constitutionally mandated time allotted to publicly present and debate the causes of their respective election contestation. Instead, the process was cancelled and those who sought their constitutional guarantees to present their grievances were silenced and accused of crimes. President Trump would not have an opportunity to respond as Twitter, which had been his main vehicle of communication, censored his tweets on that day. The hallmarks of a coup d'état are that the plotters seize the governing body and effectively silence the head of state. I would suggest, due to the failure of the system, that the question of whether the election was stolen, and the question as to whether there was a concertized effort to do so, will never likely be clarified.

We will never likely get to the bottom of what exactly happened in terms of the Capitol incursion itself. The first classic question that any investigation into any crime askes is que bono, who benefits? Certainly, Trump and his team lost big time by the Capitol incursion as the result was that the hearings that would have likely vindicated the claim that the election had been stolen were permanently interrupted and stopped. Trump also lost because such an outrage as the storming of the Capitol building could only look bad and could only feed into a false narrative that the supporters of Trump were at least uncouth if not violent. Indeed, this narrative about Trump and his supporters effectively turned attention away from the support they had offered to Antifa and elements of BLM as they looted black businesses and burned predominantly black neighborhoods as they unleashed violent terror against black citizens and as they desecrated federal and state property, including the Mark Hatfield Federal Courthouse in Portland, Oregon. Antifa essentially serves as the shock troops, to use a term coined by V. I. Lenin to describe CHEKA, the private militia of the Bolsheviks, for the Democratic Party.

Questions remain in terms of whether the protesters were allowed into the Capitol, who might have allowed them in and why, and whether the incursion could have been prevented. Questions remain in terms of whether Antifa, or perhaps other Democratic Party groups or activists might have infiltrated the crowd disguised as Trump supporters. In the initial coverage, the news media falsely asserted that President Trump, speaking at the peaceful protest rally a half a mile away, where up to a half a million people, mostly families, had gathered at the National Mall, had called for the storming of the Capitol. It was later revealed, after the damage was done to the presidents reputation, that the Capitol incursion was already well underway before the president had finished delivering his speech where he said: *I know that everyone here will soon be marching over to the Capitol building to peacefully and patriotically make your voices heard.* President Trump, perhaps later than he should have, called out the National Guard and reminded the protesters that *we are the party of law and order.*

I would argue, based upon my personal experience as a close observer of events and based on my gut, that there is evidence, from eye-witnesses, from videos and from photos, to indicate that the Capitol incursion was at least influenced by Antifa and perhaps other pro-Democratic conspirators disguised as Trump supporters. Unquestionably, real Trump supporters followed the instigators in, and some very well may have been swept up by the pent-up emotion of the event, but I nevertheless stand by my assertion that this was a planned inside job. Indeed, many conservative commentators, including me, had warned potential attendees of the peaceful rally that they might be infiltrated by Antifa, dressed in Trump garb, who might try to instigate violence. No one, other than of course the witting participants and possible conspirators, could have predicted the nature of the anticipated action. I contend that the operation was likely aided and abetted by some security personnel operating inside the Capitol. Among many credible sources, Pamela Geller published a great compendium of photos, copies of tweets, videos and news links that seem to indicate that this was the case. (3.)

And so, it begins.

Wednesday, January 6, 2021, is a date that should be remembered as one by which American politics took a major turn for the worse.

The incursion into the US Capitol building, which was mostly conducted by a motley crew of guys in Halloween costumes, would prove to be an event which would effectively slam the door on any public hearing of evidence of voter fraud in seven contested states. The whole miserable and regrettable Capital incursion fiasco, where 4 Trump supporters died, was effectively turned around and dropped onto the head of President Trump and his movement as, in classic communist agit-prop style, Trump and his movement were now to be blamed and denounced. Now, suddenly, President Trump and his supporters could, at long last, be portrayed as violent, disloyal to law and order, unpatriotic and insurrectionist. Windbag left-wing commentators, with their phony British accents and their odor of pseudo-intellectualism, could now drone on interminably with such garbage as comparing the Capital incursion to the terrorist attack of September 11, 2001 and to Pearl Harbor.

The Orwellian memory hole would reach breaking point as videos, tweets, and interminable articles written by those who had extolled the virtues of Antifa and BLM during the previous months, at a time when those Democratic Party shock troops were cutting a fiery swath of death and destruction across predominantly black neighborhoods and businesses, would disappear. Remarks by such luminaries of the establishment left as then Senator Kamala Harris and Representative Ayanna Pressley urging on the violent protesters would suddenly vanish. The looting of the Mark Hatfield Federal Courthouse in Portland, Oregon, the violent occupation of a neighborhood in Seattle, the desecration of statues across the country including the Robert Gould Shaw Memorial in Boston would soon be forgotten.

Donald Trump would fall victim to a cacophony of concocted and sanctioned conspiracy theories that were in many ways worse than the one that had hobbled 3 years of his brilliant presidency, the one that had claimed that he was a spy for Russia. Trump would now be accused of trying to overthrow the government and of such outrages as participating in a plot to murder Vice President Pence and Democratic members of Congress. Republican congressman and senators who had supported the constitutional process of hearing the evidence of voter fraud in 7 states were to be accused of sedition and any one of the 75 million citizens who voted for Trump, anyone of us who might have questioned the validity of the election now might be denounced as seditionists, as conspiracy theorists and as white supremacists.

Speaker of the House Nancy Pelosi, capitalizing on the events of the day, immediately stated that if President Trump were not toppled from office under the 25th Amendment, Congress would go forward with impeachment. The enemies of Trump had been calling for him to be removed from office under the 25th Amendment since the day he entered office. This call should be viewed in the context of classic leftism as any person or any group, in the minds and in the cant of the left, is to essentially be viewed as to be insane. This constitutes an example of psychological projection on a mass scale. Leftists, operating within what could be described as an informal mass cult, and in order to perpetuate their own myths and iron-clad opinions, must shut out the outside world lest a bit of truth might seep in and erode the iron cage that they have built around their own minds. Thus, anyone who does not goose-step in their direction is fair game to be attacked and denounced as insane.

On January 6th, America openly and decisively turned in the direction of fascism with the censorship of President Trump's Twitter account. On the day of the Capitol incursion, Trump had tweeted out a call for peace and a plea to the protestors to keep in mind the best tendencies of his movement and that the rally was meant as a peaceful free speech expression of support for the contested states in their attempt to conduct their constitutional right to contest their respective elections. That tweet was censored by Twitter and that particular act of censorship, among other coincidences of that day, raise questions regarding the possibility that the whole affair very well might have constituted a Democratic Party silent Putsch.

Trump's Twitter account would be permanently shut down as part of a purge along with those of other opponents of the new regime including Attorney Sidney Powell and Lieutenant General Michael Flynn. The Parlor app, which was one of the fastest growing apps in the country and which was taking on Facebook and Twitter, would be taken down by Apple, Google and Amazon. Parlor would be falsely accused of promoting violence at a time when Twitter allowed a *"Hang Mike Pence"* meme to go viral and while Twitter and Facebook draw considerable revenue from porn and child exploitation. The purge of Parlor, which, it should be noted, maintained more vigorous standards of banning violence than Twitter, meant that people who had built up hundreds of thousands of followers on Parlor, followers that could be instantly reached, would now be purged and dropped down the memory hole. A substantial amount of evidence and congressional testimony indicates that the big tech social networks had been shadow-banning conservatives for years. Now, with Joe Biden confirmed, the shackles would come off and big tech would go ahead and censor the President of the United States and others to whom they disagreed with politically.

As mentioned earlier, this action on the part of big tech is the very essence of fascism. Big Tech would henceforth work informally, but would nevertheless work hand in glove, with the newly installed government. The only reason why they knew they could get away with such outrageous and un-American acts of censorship is because they knew that they were acting in the interests of the new regime and, as such, the new regime would nod and look the other way. The securing by the Democrats of the US Senate, due to a special runoff election in Georgia, an election that was as questionable and likely as corrupt as was the presidential election in that state, would further lead to a consolidation of power by an unholy combination of a ruling oligarchy informally colluding with select private corporations with both working toward the same goals.

And…so we move forward.

Joseph R. Biden Jr. and Kamala D. Harris have now been inaugurated and they are now the President and the Vice President of the United States. Even though, I argue, there is overwhelming evidence that the election had been stolen from President Donald J. Trump, I nevertheless recognize Biden and Harris as President and Vice President. I mourn over what I contend was a stolen election and I am saddened and concerned over the squandered opportunity that a second Trump Administration would have otherwise offered this country and society. I believe in the American system and, as such, I support a continuity in our government which means that, however it came about, whoever was inaugurated at noon on January 20th, 2021 is the President and the Vice President. Having noted this fact, I will nevertheless not be silenced.

I believe in the American system. The 2020 election resulted in Republicans winning across the board on the local and state level, Republicans winning at least two state legislatures which now hold Republican majorities, and Republicans won almost every 2020 congressional race meaning that the Democrats now hold onto Congress by a mere thread. In the global sense, the Trump movement, as Trump received 75 million known votes and possibly millions more, should be viewed as part of a progressive international movement toward national sovereignty and human rights. The American people witnessed, in real time and out in the open, the most corrupt election in American history and it is not going to be so easy for the censorious globalist liberal establishment to lock that memory away. Indeed, in various forms, and in spite of the hatred and the scorn that will no doubt be heaped on the heads of the truth tellers, the truth will nevertheless come out, most likely this year. I am confident that truth will prevail in the end because I am confident in America.

As this book goes to press, there are several ongoing investigations into voter fraud, and I believe that these investigations will pick up steam as the year 2021 progresses. (2.) The Supreme Court has agreed to hear three cases that deal with the question of the legality of state Governors and Secretaries of States changing election laws without state legislative approval. Decisions on those cases by the Supreme Court will probably not be rendered until late in 2021 and none of those cases deal directly with voter fraud itself. Nevertheless, those cases are solid, as they pertain to a violation of the literal language of the US Constitution by those corrupt state governments, which means that the Supreme Court would have to stoop to an unprecedented level of corruption to find otherwise.

The social media censorship, which constitutes an informal form of worldwide technocratic fascism, will not stand for long in this free country. I predict that Parlor will come back on its own server and other competitors to the big tech titans will begin to spring up. Former President Trump is himself reportedly considering establishing an alternative social media site. Mike Lindell, the Pillow Guy, after being banned by Twitter and other big tech platforms for presenting evidence of voter fraud, had the resources to create his own media event which went viral along with a massive increase in pillow sales after his product was banned by the big box stores. We are witnessing the development of a parallel economy and a parallel culture and, assuming as I do that the election was stolen and that, as such, the numbers are there, we will begin to gradually overwhelm the controlling interests over time. The American counter-revolution, which is part of an organic, diverse and worldwide movement, will not be stopped.

Ending where I started

I began this short treatise, and I will end this short treatise with an expression of concern over what I contend are manifestations in America, enhanced by the events of 2021, of a slow slide down in the direction of soft Nazism. Those manifestations, I would contend, are not as severe as those that engulfed Germany with the election of Adolf Hitler as Chancellor of Germany in 1933, nor do I believe that we will likely fall to such depths. Unlike Nazi Germany, which was racially and ethnically homogenous with one significant minority, the Jews, America is a multi-racial and a multi-ethnic society which means that unlike in Germany, no particular race or ethnicity is likely to claim dominance. This is enhanced by the fact that the resistance to any such move, the Trump supporters, the MAGA movement, the so-called deplorables, we are a multi-racial and multi-ethnic group. Indeed, the propaganda by the liberal elite that the Trump resistance is white supremacist, an idiom of propaganda which itself is indicative of a trend toward Nazism by employing the classic tactic of the big lie, has not worked and it will not likely fly regardless of their dominance over the main institutions of culture and media.

I am concerned that the enthronement and the installation of the Joe Biden Administration represents the establishment of a soft National Socialist State. Let me differentiate between the type of nationalism that Biden represents and the type of nationalism that Trump and his followers support. This differentiation becomes particularly important in these times as the Biden form is glorified and has gathered a type of strength that emanates from fiat power while the Trump form is demonized. Biden represents the type of nationalism that worships, one that indeed venerates the apparatus of the state as a godless redemptive force, as a vehicle to be employed, through both overt and subtle forms of coercion, as a means to change human nature. Biden's nationalist state requires a hyper-active leadership, in the form of a strong man or a semi-secretive cabal of self-appointed so-called enlightened avatars, which is specifically the Biden model, that attempts to interject itself into all aspects of the lives of the citizen. In this endeavor, the controllers will often sincerely believe that they act in the best interests of the citizen.

The Trump model of nationalism, in contrast, and in spite of the propaganda and the lies that were directed against it by the other side, constitutes support for a limited state operating within the confines of a constitution that separates powers so as to better preserve, protect and defend individual liberty. The Trump model recognizes God, or for atheists one can replace belief in God with that of objective nature, as the sovereign source of rights and of reality itself. In this model, nature and natures God, to coin a phrase employed by Thomas Jefferson in the American

Declaration of Independence, is the source of sovereignty. God, the great sovereign, grants a limited degree of sovereignty to every man and women as both men and women are, according to the Bible, created by him equally and in his image. Indeed, Donald Trump captured the essence of his brand of nationalism in his remarkable Inaugural Address, a text that should be read and understood by all Americans. He stated: *today we are not merely transferring power from one administration to another, or from one party to another, but we are transferring power from Washington, D.C., and giving it back to you, the people.* (1.)

The Joe Biden Administration started with a bang as, on day one, Biden signed 17 executive orders. Evidence suggests that the orders signed by President Joe Biden were vetted by outgoing Attorney General Bill Barr operating behind Trumps back. The original constitutional authority for the president to issue executive orders had been to apply such laws either to the executive branch or for more ceremonial functions. President George Washington had, for example, issued an executive order recognizing Thanksgiving as a national holiday by which the nation would express thanks to God. President Ulysses S. Grant issued an executive order in 1870 recognizing Christmas as a national holiday. When President Abraham Lincoln issued the Emancipation Proclamation as an executive order, he did so with the understanding that such a proclamation, existing as it did outside the purview of the executive branch, would eventually need ratification by Congress and this occurred with the passage of the 13th Amendment to the Constitution two years later.

The expansion of executive orders began in 1933 when Congress authorized emergency powers in the first week of the Franklin D. Roosevelt Administration in response to the depression. These powers, which began a gradual process that has continued ever since, resulted in stronger powers in the hands of the president. FDR used those emergency powers to close all banks, what is known as the Bank Holiday, confiscate all gold coins, and eventually set up the so-called alphabet bureaucracies. These measures continued a trend that had gotten under way in earnest during the Woodrow Wilson Administration which was the transfer of governing powers from Congress and the States to unelected and autonomous bureaus which would increasingly assume semi-sovereign powers.

Biden, upon entering office, indicated that he intended to further expand those powers and the speed and depth of his executive orders so far indicate that the expansion would further render the elected Congress and, as such, the US Constitution less relevant. With a stroke of a pen, Biden eliminated over ten thousand jobs with the irrational cancelling of the Keystone Pipeline. This measure, which endangers the environment as Canadian oil would now have to cross into the

US by train and truck, would essentially be a gift to the oil companies and might contribute toward undoing Trump policies that led to energy independence. This one act, which would likely lead to the loss of upwards of a hundred thousand jobs in aggregate, would likely contribute to a raise in the cost of oil which hurts production and potentially raises prices thus hurting working people.

Other executive orders included rejoining the Paris Climate Accord, an agreement which could negatively effect energy production in the United States and the western democracies while letting Russia and China off the hook and an order to use taxpayer money to pressure conservative nations to permit abortions. These executive orders, done without the benefit of debate and without a vote in Congress and, as such, without a public hearing or the consent of the people, would represent a considerable expansion and further centralization of presidential powers. Biden has let it be known that he intends to govern by executive order if Congress does not cooperate.

Indications are that Biden intends, according to remarks made within his inner circle, to undo President Trump's America first policies. America First has been mislabeled by its opponents as Fascist, but the exact opposite is the case. The America First movement was the peace or the non-interventionist movement that existed before America entered WW II, a movement that disappeared after Japan bombed Pearl Harbor on December 7, 1941. America First included those both on the left and on the right with the communist left switching sides after Hitler double-crossed his communist ally Stalin and invaded Russia on June 6, 1940 in what is known as Operation Barbarossa. Literally overnight, the American communist left, having been anti-war when it served the interest of Stalin and Hitler, became pro-war and would pose as super patriotic. The American communists and their fellow travelers then proceeded to demonize America First, which was still the peace party that included both liberals and conservatives, as pro-Hitler.

It is perfectly natural for a nation to put the interests of its own citizens first over those of other nations. Indeed, this is the very reason why nations exist in the first place. This principle is understood by the animal and even by the plant kingdom. This is a normal and natural part of being alive. President Trump sought to restore this natural policy by re-negotiating trade agreements to favor American industry and labor, by reducing American involvement in foreign wars, and by putting in place favorable business policies so as to help domestic production and, as such, to lift segments of the American population out of poverty. The return by Biden to policies of perpetual war, high taxes, trade and energy deficits, enmeshment in the New World Order or what is now being called the Great Reset, are all policies that advance the interests of the unelected government in collusion with select corporations and this, dear reader, represents the very essence of fascism.

The rise of fascism under Biden is emerging in our culture as well. Individuals and organizations are now being routinely de-platformed, bank accounts are being suspended, jobs are being denied and people are being marginalized and shunned by this growing tyrannical trend. This is not, at least not yet, comparable in its severity or formality to the early period of the Nazi regime in Germany, not in the literal sense, but the philosophy and politics is exactly analogous. A few days before the Biden inauguration, as an example, over 500 people in the publishing industry signed a letter committing themselves to not publishing anything created by Trump or anyone affiliated with his administration. Signatories included DC Comics President Paul Levitz, journalist Sarah Weinman and author Celeste Ng. (2.)

In one of his initial executive orders, President Biden removed the 1776 Commission Report, which presents patriotic guidelines for public education in terms of teaching American history. The report had been falsely denounced by leftists as racist because the report rejects critical race theory as the best modality for education. Critical race theory advances Marxist principles originally patented by Marxist theoretician Franz Fanon, the author of The Wretched of the Earth, and by Harvard Professor Charles Pierce, which would effectively put anyone who fails to genuflect to the left under a microscope in an attempt to find anything that might indicate racism. What they do not find, they can make it up with pseudo psychological jargon while giving their allies a pass. This form of tyranny avoids any real conversation on racial disparity as such a conversation might risk exposing the damage that leftist policies and ideas have wracked upon the African-American community since the 1060's.

Certainly, many liberal establishment voices are intoning ideas that can only be described as Fascist. Former newswoman Katie Couric, during an appearance on Real Time with Bill Maher, said: *The question is how are we going to really almost deprogram these people who have signed up for the cult of Trump.* Couric was echoing a call by Washington Post columnist Eugene Robinson who stated during an appearance on MSNBC: *there are millions of Americans, almost all White, almost all Republicans, who somehow need to be deprogrammed* as he refered to *a Trumpist cult.* (3.) Novelist and leftist activist Don Winslow is promoting a video which alls upon citizens to become cyber-detectives to monitor and report to authorities their neighbors, colleagues, friends and family members who might be Trump supporters. (4.)

In a chilling video, one which has already received 3.5 million views, the narrator, in a manner reminiscent of a Nazi Gauleiter, states the following:

The greatest threat facing America today comes from within: radical extreme conservatives, also known as domestic terrorists. They're hidden among us, disguised behind regular jobs. They are your children's teachers. They work at supermarkets, malls, doctor's offices, and many are police officers and soldiers.

The Gestapo style narrative continues:

I'm proposing we form a citizen army," he says. "Our weapons will be computers and cell phones. We who are monitoring extremists on the internet and reporting their findings to authorities.

The video then prods future goose-steppers to utilize their computers in their spying which he compares to the discovery of Osama Ben Laden whom he compares, by proxy, to Trump and his supporters:

Remember, before the Navy SEALs killed Osama bin Laden he had to be found," the clip continues. "He was found by a CIA analyst working on a computer thousands of miles away. (5.)

I could go on and on, almost as infinitum, and my hope, going forward, that I am able to go on, that I am allowed to go on in this threatening atmosphere. I will conclude this short treatise with the simple observation that these fascist ideas are not being promoted by some fringe extreme group but, rather, these ideas have now been successfully launched and they are sanctioned by an administration that benefits from them, one that is in harmony with them and with their goals. This dangerous, hateful, un-American agenda has been ramped up in these times and yet, with Donald Trump now driven out of office, these ideas are in many ways more dangerous and insidious as the fever pitch of the daily drip…drip…drip has been muted out of circumstance and in response to present conditions. I hear this drumbeat every day as my own YouTube videos are deleted and as my YouTube channel is demonetized. Every day, I turn on the station, preparing to do my daily live stream interview, never knowing if this is the day that they have finally decided to pull the plug.

The drumbeat is growing louder with each passing day.

Notes

The War against Trump

1. <u>The Sociological Imagination</u>: Chapter 1, The Promise, C. Wright Mills, Oxford University Press, New York, 1959.: p. 21: Mills: I am hopeful of course that all my own biases will show, for I think judgements should be explicit…. Let those who do not care for mine use their rejections to them to make their own as explicit and as acknowledged as I am going to try to make mine!

2. Ibid. p.3 Neither the life of an individual nor the history of a society can be understood without understanding both.0

3. <u>Bush Derangement Syndrome</u>: Charles Krauthammer, Townhall, December 5, 2003. Krauthammer: Bush Derangement Syndrome: the acute onset of paranoia in otherwise normal people in reaction to the policies, the presidency -- nay -- the very existence of George W. Bush.

4. The Sociological Imagination. P. 4.

5. <u>The Pseudo-Science of Microaggressions</u>, Althea Nagai, National Association of Scholars, Spring 2017 edition.

6. <u>The Education of Henry Adams</u>, Henry Adams, 1907: Politics, as a practice, whatever its professions, had always been the systematic organization of hatreds, and Massachusetts politics had been as harsh as the climate.

7. <u>'The Hate Is Real': Black Georgia Lawmaker Says She Was Berated at Supermarket</u>, Audra Melton, The New York Times, July 21, 2019 p. 1.

8. <u>The Campaign to impeach President Trump has begun</u>, Matea Gold, The Washington Post, January 20, 2017.

The Capitol Incursion and the Reichstag Fire

1. <u>About half of Republicans don't think Joe Biden should be sworn in as president</u>, A new Vox/DFP Poll finds that most Republicans are still questioning the election results, Li Zhou, VOX, Jan. 11, 2021

2. <u>Trump urges Pence to send Electoral Results Back to State Legislatures</u>, Jack Phillips, The Epoch Times, January 6, 2021

3. <u>Photos, reports show ANTIFA infiltrators stormed the Capitol building</u>. Pamela Geller, Geller Report, January 6, 2021

And so, it begins.

1. <u>Twitter allows "Hang Mike Pence" to trend while banning President Trump for inciting violence.</u> Pamela Geller, The Geller Report, Jan. 9, 2021

2. <u>Report: A group of 400 Former US Intelligence Officials are Investigating "Blatant" Election Fraud</u>. Victoria Taft, PJ Media, Jan. 3, 2021

Ending where I started

1. <u>Inaugural Address: President Donald J. Trump, January 20, 2017</u>

2. <u>Over 500 Fascists in Book Industry sign letter demanding no publisher offer book deal to Trump or his admin.</u> Pamela Geller, The Geller Report, January 19, 2021.

3. <u>Liberal Media, Big Tech calls to "deprogram" deplatform Trump supporters</u>, David Rutz, Fox News, January 17, 2021

4. <u>Left Calls for Army of Citizen Detectives to Monitor and Report Trump Supporters</u>, Joshua Klein, Breitbart, January 19, 2021

5. Ibid.